Everything You Always Wanted to Know About PUBERTY

—and Shouldn't Learn on TikTok

FOR CURIOUS GIRLS

BY GEMMA HONG & SOPHIE YOUNG

ILLUSTRATED BY AMELIA PINNEY

downtown bookworks

downtown bookworks

Downtown Bookworks Inc.
New York, New York
www.downtownbookworks.com

Special thanks to Althea Lasseter

For my awesome
mother, who succeeded in
raising an awesome daughter,
and my awesome grandmother,
who succeeded in raising an
awesome granddaughter.
It runs in the family.
—GEMMA

For my Mom—
thank you for your
kindness, love, and patience,
especially during my puberty
years. Except for that time
when I was 12 and shaved my legs
for the first time and you put
a picture of it in one of your
scrapbooks. Not cool.
—SOPHIE

Thank you to my
dad for always supporting
my creative endeavors, my sisters
who stood by my side through all
the childhood temper tantrums, and
of course, to my mom for showing me
what an empowered woman looks like.
—AMELIA

what's in this book

PART 1

PART 2

PART 3

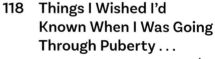

foreword

This isn't the puberty lesson you learned from your creepy middle school health teacher by watching an ancient video of animated eggs. We aren't doctors or textbook writers, and we are barely older than you. We just made it out the other side of puberty ourselves. We remember it well, along with the exhilaration, anxiety, and a desire for someone to tell us everything was going to be OK during those months when our moods changed faster than the weather.

So we got together with our publisher to show and tell you about all the wild changes your body and brain are going through. Take it from us—it's going to be fine! It's also going to be fun and exciting to transform into the grown-up woman version of yourself.

WHO WE ARE

GEMMA

I'm a GenZer, New Jerseyan, H Mart lover, fried chicken expert, chronically online Twitter user, and distinguished Korean American. I went to suburban public school until high school, when I switched to an all-girls Catholic school in New York City. I definitely couldn't ask my mom about puberty (that would've been so weird), so I figured things out together with my friends and the internet. For me, the toughest part about that time was trying to understand where

I fit in the world. Being a first-generation Korean American and suddenly moving to a fancy private high school complicated some of that, but I soldiered on. After all, I had sports bras to hunt down, bacne to fight off, and homework to finish!

I'm still peeved by random forehead pimples, but at 20, I'm far more comfortable with my body and my identity.

SOPHIE

At 19, I'm technically a grown-up who spends most of her time reading and writing about everything from stars to camping to family to puberty. But I will always be the shockingly tall bisexual kid from the foothills of South Carolina at heart. For me, puberty was about constantly growing out of every pair of pants I bought, figuring out my sexuality, and trying to find ways to get out of doing math homework.

Sometimes I still feel like a gangly teenager, but now that I'm somewhat (barely!) removed from it, I feel much more comfortable and proud of who I am and how I look. Although I still have a hard time finding pants long enough for my legs. You can't have everything.

I grew up in a very busy neighborhood in New York City, a middle child with two sisters, and daughter of a feminist mom. My dad uses a wheelchair, which made me comfortable with differences and sometimes being stared at as I walked and he rolled down the streets. I danced and made art at my artsy schools.

My friends and I taught each other everything we knew about puberty through a lot of show-and-tell. Good times!

I also struggled with mean girls, body image issues, and serious anxiety–the darker side of puberty. Those were some stressful years for me, but I learned A LOT and came out better for my struggles. Happily, I get to do the thing I love (making art) and share my stories with you.

AND...

We talked to many friends and helpful teens, and mined our own lives to bring you the views and stories in this book. We don't identify who said what or which story came from where—not because anyone is embarrassed or ashamed of their feelings or experiences—just because it makes for friendlier reading. "I" is not a single person but all of the girls and women who contributed to this book. Some were really early bloomers, others didn't go through puberty until tenth grade. Contributors run the gamut from tiny to tall, flat-chested to large-breasted, hairless to hairy. We identify as straight, bisexual, and lesbian. We've shared personal anecdotes in the hopes of connecting with as many readers as possible. Hopefully our stories are your stories too. We're all in this together!

DON'T BE SHY!

Though we've tried to be thorough, we may miss addressing something that you are going through. If you have questions that aren't answered in these pages, please talk to your sister, mother, aunt, cousin, doctor, teacher, counselor, or guardian for help if you need it. Puberty can be daunting.

You are going to learn a lot from this book, but you can always learn more from the women in your life.

HIS, HERS, AND THEIRS

The sexual organs you are assigned at birth determine your gender at birth. If you are born with a vagina, you are considered a girl, and if you're born with a penis, you're considered a boy. But not everyone feels at home in their body or identifies with the gender they are assigned at birth. Some people don't identify as a boy or girl, but as nonbinary. People who don't identify with their assigned gender are called transgender (or trans). Some people who are assigned female at birth later identify as male, and vice versa. If you are trans, you probably have a different set of concerns as you go through puberty. If you are feeling confusion about your gender, or anxiety about going through puberty, you should discuss this with a parent and/or your doctor or therapist. Many people question their gender identity, and if this is something you're experiencing, you are not alone!

That said, this book is geared toward the concerns of cis girls. While trans girls are more than welcome to learn from this book, their experiences with hormone therapy and the resulting changes would probably be better addressed elsewhere. We are using *she/her/hers* pronouns throughout the book for simplicity.

WHAT EXACTLY IS PUBERTY?

Puberty is a time of change in your life. The size and shape of your body changes a lot. Your moods and feelings shift *dramatically*. You will be looked at differently, and your place in the world may feel unfamiliar too.

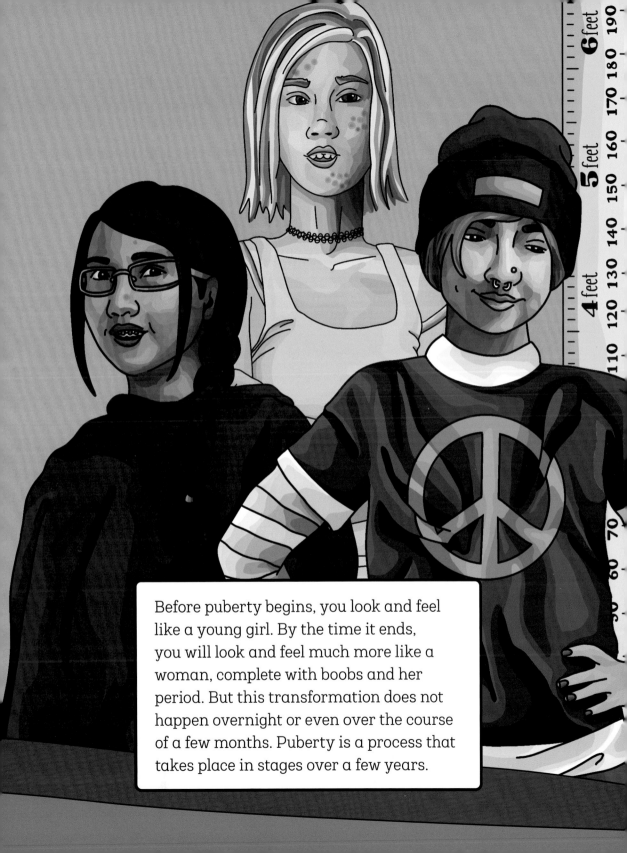

Before puberty begins, you look and feel like a young girl. By the time it ends, you will look and feel much more like a woman, complete with boobs and her period. But this transformation does not happen overnight or even over the course of a few months. Puberty is a process that takes place in stages over a few years.

For most girls, the first signs of puberty appear between the ages of 9 and 13. It's not unheard of, however, to sprout underarm hair or the beginnings of breasts earlier or later.

FIRST THINGS FIRST

For most girls, the first sign of puberty is the appearance of breast buds or strange new sensations in their nipples. Some girls will grow pubic hair before their breasts develop. Other girls notice their body odor changing before anything else happens. From then on, the stages tend to follow the same general order though it's not like the whistle blows and everyone dives into the pool at the same time. The age estimates for each stage are just averages. There is nothing wrong with you if you don't get breast buds until you're 16 or if you grew your first pubic hair at 8. At the end of this ride, you will definitely be a fully grown woman.

Whoa?!

STAGE 1
around ages 9–11

- Breast buds begin to form. These are tiny bumps about the size of a nickel that grow underneath your nipple.
- Pubic hair begins to grow.
- The skin around your nipples may darken.

We're legit budding!

STAGE 3
around ages 13–14

- You will most likely get your first period!
- Your pubic hair grows thicker and spreads

Hellooo pit hair!

STAGE 2
around ages 11–12

- Your breasts grow fuller.
- Hair grows under your armpits.
- Your figure fills out—your hips and thighs start to look curvier.
- You will start to have a growth spurt during this time.

STAGE 4
around age 15 and up

- Your period becomes more regular.
- Your growth slows down.
- Your breasts also stop growing, settling into their adult size.

KNOCK, KNOCK

Who's there?

HORMONES!

Your hips and breasts don't just decide on their own to fill out. Zits don't appear out of nowhere, and neither do your swingy moods. Hormones are behind every change your body and brain experience during puberty. Here's how it works (the short version):

About a year before you even notice anything different in your body, your brain is getting things ready. The hypothalamus, an area deep in your brain that acts as the body's command center, starts to release a few different hormones. Hormones are chemicals produced in your body that control what certain cells and organs do. The first round of hormones to be released is called gonadotropin-releasing hormones. Don't even try—we'll call them GnRH for short. GnRH finds its way to the pituitary gland, a pea-sized gland in your brain not too far from the hypothalamus.

The hormones and pituitary gland act together to let the body know it's time to start developing. They need more hormone helpers to make this happen. So next up, the GnRH and pituitary gland release two more hormones: lutenizing hormone (LH) and follicle-stimulating hormone (FSH).

But wait—there's more! Then the LH and FSH trigger the production of still more hormones. This time, the hormones estrogen and progesterone are released in the ovaries.

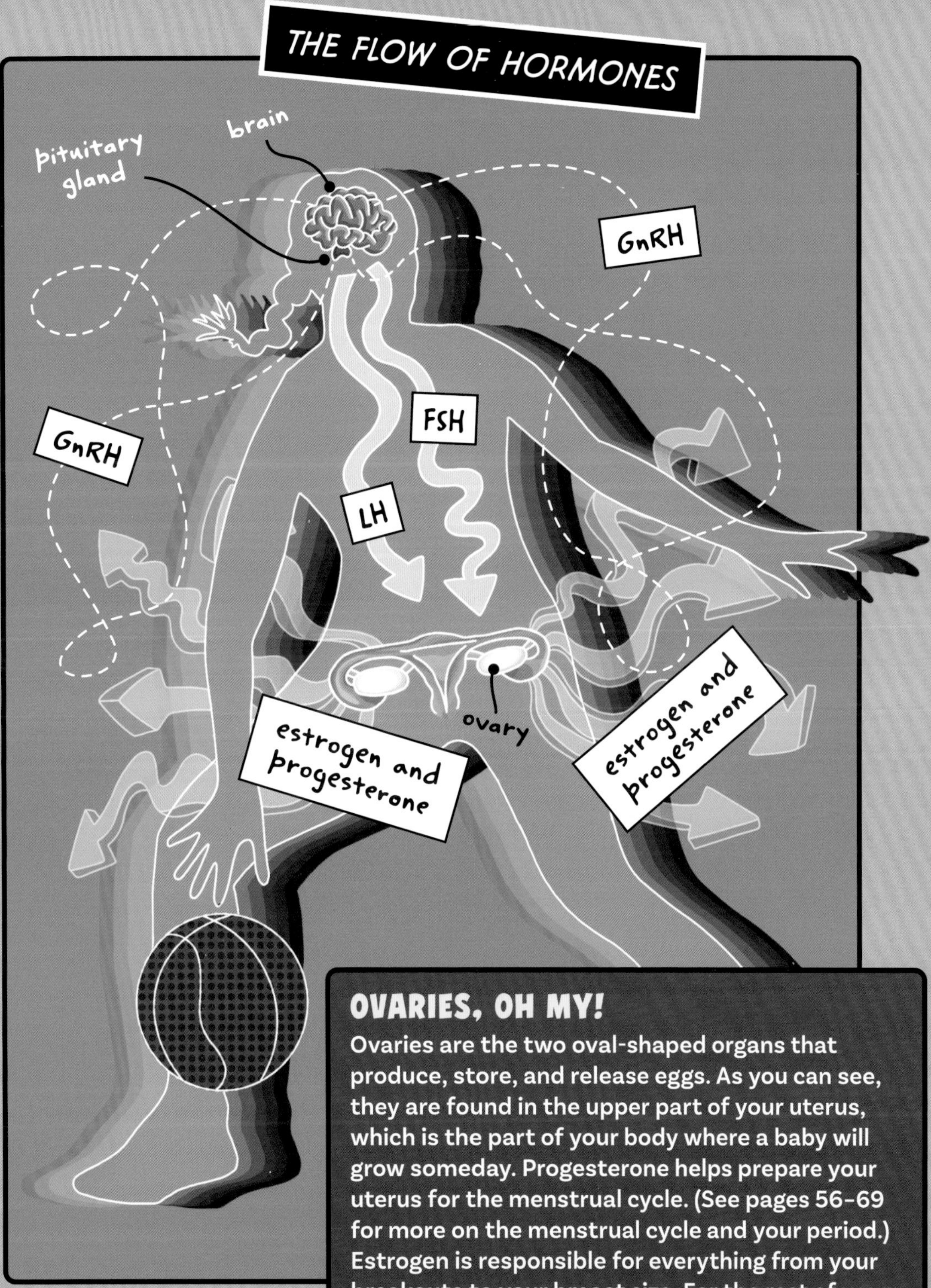

pituitary gland

brain

GnRH

GnRH

FSH

LH

ovary

estrogen and progesterone

estrogen and progesterone

OVARIES, OH MY!

Ovaries are the two oval-shaped organs that produce, store, and release eggs. As you can see, they are found in the upper part of your uterus, which is the part of your body where a baby will grow someday. Progesterone helps prepare your uterus for the menstrual cycle. (See pages 56–69 for more on the menstrual cycle and your period.) Estrogen is responsible for everything from your breakouts to your breast size. For the rest of your life, your estrogen levels will impact your health and moods and so much more.

WELCOME TO YOUR NEW BODY!

Not since you were a baby outgrowing your onesies every few weeks have you experienced the kind of extreme transformation you will undergo during puberty. In my house, my parents tracked our height on a wall in the kitchen. Up until I turned 11, the lines for each year are all about two inches apart. Then there are these huge gaps—three or four inches—between the marks for three years. I knew things were changing. But seeing it on that wall made it so real and obvious.

Part 1 of this book covers growth and many of the other changes happening on the outside of your body.

The GROWTH Spurt

One of the most obvious outward signs of puberty is how much you're growing. It seems like one morning you wake up and get dressed and your favorite pair of jeans have become capris. Don't worry—nobody snuck into your house and shrunk all your clothes. It means your growth spurt has begun.

A growth spurt is exactly what it sounds like: you're growing A LOT in a shortish period of time. From the time you're about four years old until you hit puberty, most people grow about two inches a year. Totally reasonable pace. But then, sometime between the ages of 9 and 14, BAM, you start growing at least three inches a year. You'll have one to two years of this supercharged growth, during which you will also be outgrowing your shoes in record time. Some people even experience growing pains, usually in the legs. In the 6 to 12 months before you start menstruating, your growth speeds up even more, and then your period throws the hammer down. Party's over. After your period, you'll typically only grow about two or three more inches in total before reaching your adult height.

GETTING ALL TRIPPED UP?

Your arms, legs, hands, and feet grow faster than your trunk, which is why adolescents can look a bit gangly and awkward. When you're growing faster than a TikTok trend, coordination tends to go out the window. Don't worry, it'll come back once you get used to your new center of gravity.

When Did You Get So TALL?

HEY, WAIT UP!

Some girls hit their growth spurt a lot earlier than others (I knew a girl in sixth grade who was already 5 foot 8!), and some take a bit longer. Some girls get their periods on the early side, and their growth may slow down earlier too. Other people, like me, seem to keep on growing. I didn't start menstruating until I was 15, and I kept on growing until I was 17 years old and 6 foot 2! Don't worry if you feel like you're much shorter or taller than your friends. By eighth grade, I was taller than all my teachers, including the men. I also had a friend who was just 4 foot 11. People come in all different shapes and sizes.

There are no hard rules in terms of how tall you will be or when you will reach that height. Your adult height is determined by genetics and nutrition. But one thing is for sure during those middle school years: the boys in your class will seem shorter. Girls usually go through puberty a few years before boys do, and girls' growth spurts come earlier too. It can be awkward—or kind of fun! Take advantage of that head start as much as you can. Destroy the boys in basketball and volleyball. I have a twin brother, and I loved towering over him while I could. Now he's 6 foot 8!

YOU'RE GETTING SLEEPY...

Shooting up three-plus inches a year can be exhausting work. Before puberty, I was up at 7 a.m. on weekend mornings watching Cartoon Network. In eighth grade when my growth spurt hit, I had to set six alarms just to make sure I got up on time for school. How dare anyone wake me before noon? What cruel, cruel person decided school should start so early? Your body is so busy growing, you may feel exhausted all the time. You might need to nap like a baby after school or go to sleep earlier on school nights. You may spend most of your weekend in bed. This is not laziness, it's growing.

Most growing actually happens in your sleep, when the human growth hormone levels in your body peak. You've probably been annoyed to hear from some grown-up that you need to get plenty of sleep and eat well so that you'll grow tall. It's actually true.

Honey? Time for dinner!

Head, Shoulders, BOOBS & HIPS

The biological reason your body changes shape is that it's preparing to have a baby *someday*. Your body needs a certain amount of fat in order to ovulate, so you start to store a little bit of fat around your hips. (Check out pages 56–59 for more info on ovulation.) The mammary glands in your breasts develop to their adult size so that they can produce milk for a future baby. Don't worry! This doesn't happen if you're not pregnant. Your body is just getting ready in advance. So even though you are way too young to think about having a baby, your body is preparing. That's what puberty is about.

Your body grows up and out, basically in every direction during puberty. Even your skeleton changes! Your bones get stronger, and some bones will thicken as they lengthen. On the outside, this will look like your hips getting wider and your thighs may spread out. There are some big changes going on!

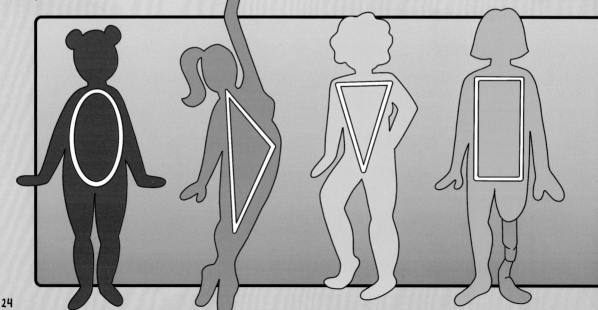

WEIGHT CHANGES? WORRY NOT.

As your hormone levels surge, you might also start gaining weight more easily. You may discover that your favorite shorts from last summer don't get past your knees now. You might eat and exercise about the same as you did before puberty, but now you are packing on some pounds. This happened to me! Even though I still played soccer year-round and ate the same size meals and types of snacks that I always did, I gained some chub during middle school and high school. One of my middle school friends ate so much we called her "The Human Vacuum." She was going through her growth spurt and also playing competitive volleyball every day. That takes a lot of fuel! Weight gain is natural and healthy during this stage. Some girls will see a big spike in appetite. And some girls just stretch out like taffy. As long as you keep exercising and eating healthy, some weight gain during puberty is to be expected and is absolutely nothing to worry about.

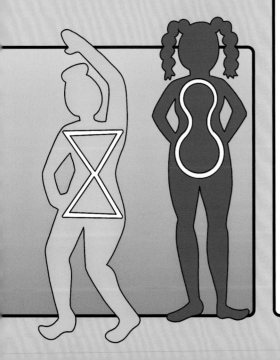

EMBRACE THE CHANGE

Change can be uncomfortable, and you might miss your favorite leggings or the tank top that won't stretch over your postpuberty boobs. Do what makes you confident and happy, whether that's finding new clothes that suit your changing body or experimenting with a funky haircut or color. The way you look today is not the way you'll look in five months or five years from now, but try to love your body every step of the way anyway.

Eating WELL

YES protein, fruit & vegetables.

Because your body is working so hard during these years (it's not easy growing boobs and body hair!), it's important to give it hard-working food. You will also feel better if you eat well. You'll have more energy, and won't be as moody if you pay attention and make good choices. You are like a hibernating bear filling up for a good long sleep. Eat, sleep, grow. Repeat. That is puberty.

Not so much with the junk food.

WHAT ARE GOOD CHOICES?

You can't go wrong with protein (lean meat, eggs, beans, nuts), fruit, and vegetables. And drink plenty of water. Water is good for pretty much everything, but it's especially helpful for keeping teenage skin clearer.

Sometimes the body knows exactly what it needs. I couldn't drink enough milk when I was going through my growth spurt. It went straight to my bones! In addition to having a bigger appetite, a lot of girls get cravings before their period. Chocolate cravings are really common, and there's a reason for that: hormones. In the days before your period, your feel-good hormone levels drop. Sweet, fatty foods are comforting and drive up your seretonin levels, which makes you feel better. You will not be the first girl to scarf down a bag of chips or a tray of brownies when she's on her period. Just try to get back to healthy eating when you can tear yourself away from the junky stuff. Whole grains and oatmeal are much better bets.

NO MEAT, NO PROBLEM!

A lot of animal-loving girls don't eat meat at all. If you are one of those girls, good for you! The best protein sources for vegetarians are soybeans (edamame) and soy milk, lentils, Greek yogurt, peas, quinoa, nuts, and nut butters. Be sure you're getting enough.

Getting Used to Your NEW BOD

Like your first two-wheel bicycle or pair of heels, your new body may take some getting used to before you feel comfortable. I can still remember the first time I bumped into my boobs with my arms while I was running, and the way I had to lie down on my bed to pull up my jeans around my new hips. You may look in a store window and see a sort of familiar woman inside, only to realize it's your own reflection and holy cow you are the woman!

These changes can be really exciting. Trying on new, grown-up clothes can be fun, like a teenage version of dress-up. It can also be horrifying, depending on how you feel about your new shape. Experiment until you figure out what feels comfortable. And try to remember that you are the person you are dressing for. You don't need to wear what your friends are wearing or what you think your crush will like. You don't need to make yourself invisible or draw attention to yourself—unless that's what you want to do. You do need to feel good in your skin.

You may feel creeped out by the way adults start to look at you. Or boys, or other girls. My chest was perfectly flat until I was 16 and then *fully* developed in the space of one week. Not kidding—I went from just having nipples to needing a size C bra in seven days. I remember walking down the hallway in school and hearing a guy in my class yell, "Since when did you have boobs!?!?" Getting all that attention can be overwhelming. So here's what you need to do: Learn to love your powerful muscles, your bulges, your leanness, your perfect toes, your fuzzy arms, any and all of it. Know that you are beautiful just the way you are.

I HATE My Body!

The sudden weight gain and shape-shifting of puberty along with the impact of estrogen on moods make it a risky time for developing eating disorders. I took a ton of dance classes in middle school and high school. Spending hours every day looking at my reflection in a leotard and tights and then being critiqued for growing boobs or being a little bit bloated definitely took a toll on me.

BODY DYSMORPHIA AND DISORDERED EATING

Body dysmorphia describes a condition in which you think you have a major defect and can't stop focusing on the defect. People with body dysmorphia will actually see themselves in a completely unrealistic way. For example, a healthy, normal-sized person might be convinced that her thighs are enormous and disgusting. And then she might develop an eating disorder in an effort to slim down her perfectly normal thighs.

People who have **anorexia** severely limit their food intake to a point where it is unhealthy. If you were to see someone with anorexia, you would think she looked horribly, painfully skinny. But that person would see herself as obese and obsess about her weight and food.

Bulimia is a different type of eating disorder that involves binging–eating an unhealthy amount of food–followed by purging or obsessive exercising.

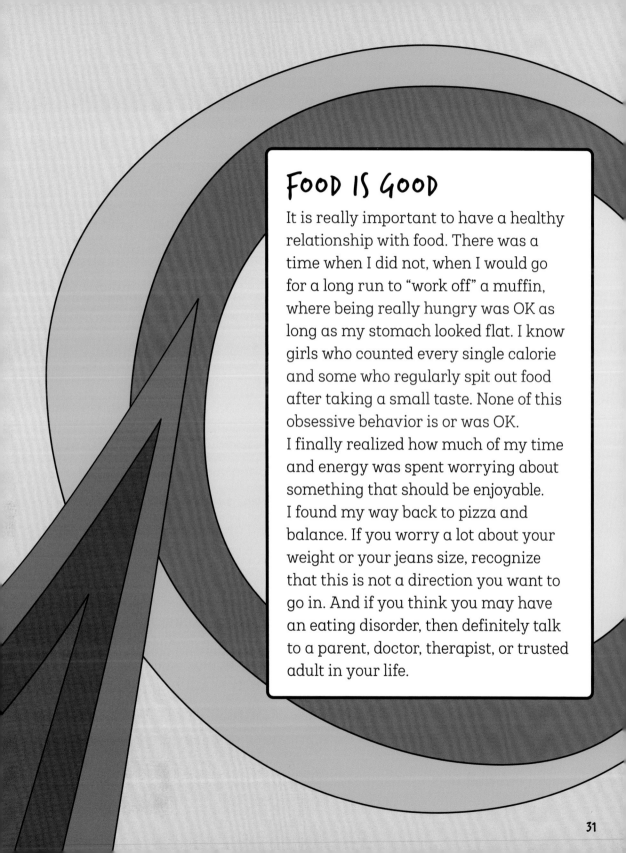

FOOD IS GOOD

It is really important to have a healthy relationship with food. There was a time when I did not, when I would go for a long run to "work off" a muffin, where being really hungry was OK as long as my stomach looked flat. I know girls who counted every single calorie and some who regularly spit out food after taking a small taste. None of this obsessive behavior is or was OK.

I finally realized how much of my time and energy was spent worrying about something that should be enjoyable. I found my way back to pizza and balance. If you worry a lot about your weight or your jeans size, recognize that this is not a direction you want to go in. And if you think you may have an eating disorder, then definitely talk to a parent, doctor, therapist, or trusted adult in your life.

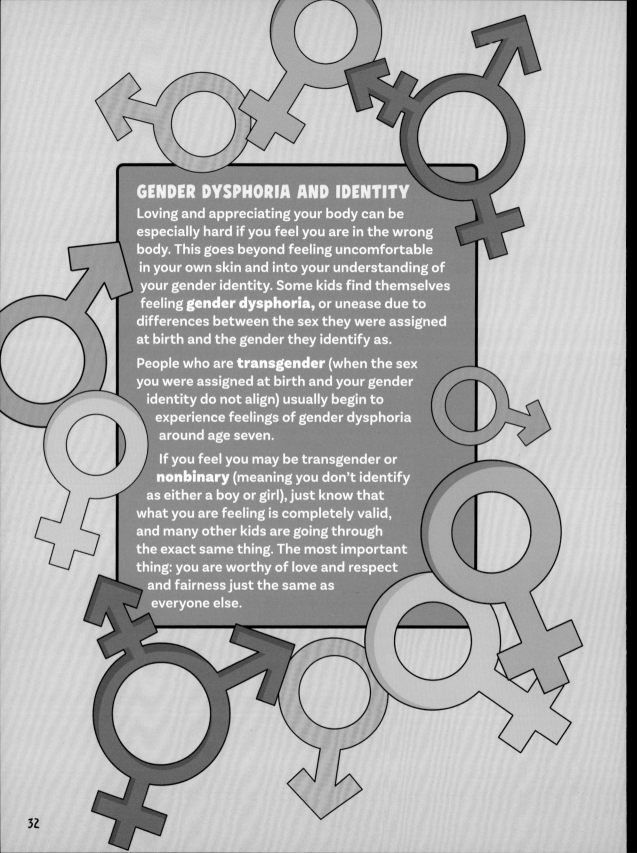

GENDER DYSPHORIA AND IDENTITY

Loving and appreciating your body can be especially hard if you feel you are in the wrong body. This goes beyond feeling uncomfortable in your own skin and into your understanding of your gender identity. Some kids find themselves feeling **gender dysphoria,** or unease due to differences between the sex they were assigned at birth and the gender they identify as.

People who are **transgender** (when the sex you were assigned at birth and your gender identity do not align) usually begin to experience feelings of gender dysphoria around age seven.

If you feel you may be transgender or **nonbinary** (meaning you don't identify as either a boy or girl), just know that what you are feeling is completely valid, and many other kids are going through the exact same thing. The most important thing: you are worthy of love and respect and fairness just the same as everyone else.

ADORNING the Body

When I was 15, I had a Pinterest board dedicated to all the tattoos (mostly koi fish for some reason) I was going to get. One of my closest friends was on her fourth hair color. Another friend got a septum piercing. I may have gone a bit crazy with eyeliner. One day you, too, might find yourself wanting to express yourself differently. Maybe a mermaid tattoo on your ankle, bright purple hair, or 17 ear piercings are the statement you want to make. And maybe next week, you'll be feeling a whole different vibe. Express yourself for sure! But while you are young and experimenting, bear in mind that some of this stuff is permanent!

Start slowly and with temporary options. Temporary tattoos are fun and painless. Henna looks great—and wears off. Spray-on temporary hair colors allow you to try out that green do before committing to it. Maybe you just want to stay completely au naturel. That's fine too! I didn't get my ears pierced until I turned 18, and as of now, no koi tattoos. And no regrets.

33

BOOBS!

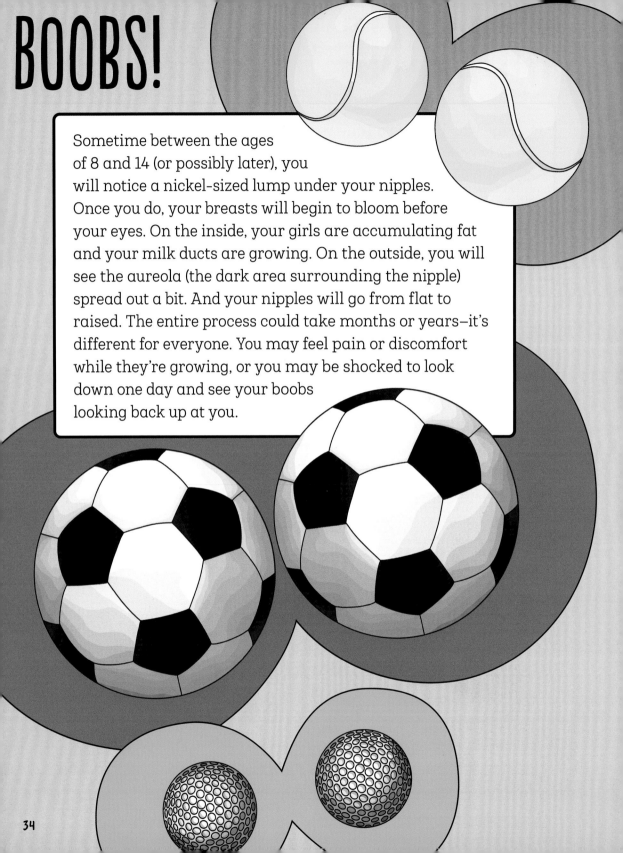

Sometime between the ages of 8 and 14 (or possibly later), you will notice a nickel-sized lump under your nipples. Once you do, your breasts will begin to bloom before your eyes. On the inside, your girls are accumulating fat and your milk ducts are growing. On the outside, you will see the aureola (the dark area surrounding the nipple) spread out a bit. And your nipples will go from flat to raised. The entire process could take months or years—it's different for everyone. You may feel pain or discomfort while they're growing, or you may be shocked to look down one day and see your boobs looking back up at you.

APPLES & ORANGES

While boobs are mostly round, the roundness as well as the size and shape varies a lot from body to body. Breasts can be perky and upright or heavy and full. They may fall close together, creating serious cleavage, or they could be wide-set enough for crumbs to slip down your shirt between them. 🙄 They could be a barely-there swelling under your nipple, ginormous orbs that make your back hurt, fleshy, firm, pointy—and everything in between.

Breasts get A LOT of attention—in fashion and media and culture, and from people who don't have them. It feels really weird when you suddenly have what seems like a whole new body part that gives you an entirely different shape. Nothing says, "I'm a woman!" to the outside world like a pair of boobs. Yup, you are becoming a woman. And soon enough, it feels normal.

NIP & TUCK

There is plenty of diversity in the world of nipples and aureolas as well. The aureola—the disk of darker skin surrounding the nipple—grows larger and darker during puberty. The whole package can range in color from pink to brown, light to dark, depending on your skintone. Most nipples become raised after puberty, but some people have inverted nipples, which means the surface is smooth. I have a friend who loves her inverted nipples because she never needs to wear a bra. It's not unheard of to have one raised and one inverted nipple. Your nipples may not look perfectly symmetrical either. All totally normal.

BRAS

Buying your first bra is a rite of passage for some girls and no big deal for others. Like most girls I know, I got my first bra before I actually needed a bra. It just suddenly felt more comfortable to have a cute, soft, stretchy training bra on under a T-shirt. It can take anywhere from a few months to a few years before you reach your full-grown size, and your feelings about bras may evolve along with your boobs. Here's what you need to know.

TO WEAR OR NOT TO WEAR

Wearing a bra should be about your comfort and confidence. A well-fitted bra can support your breasts, reduce back pain (if you have large breasts), and help you feel good about your appearance. When I exercise, I like to wear a sports bra so my boobs don't jump around. I also wear padded bras with certain outfits because I like the way they fill out my clothes.

However, I don't always want or need a bra to feel comfortable and confident. In really hot weather, an extra piece of clothing means another sweaty layer. I skip a bra if I'm wearing a sweatshirt or something loose. I never wear a bra at home, but I have friends with bigger boobs who are uncomfortable without the support of a bra. You do you!

A "Brief" INTRO

Unlike everything else you will ever wear, bra sizes include a number and a letter. The number refers to the circumference of your chest area. If you were to wrap a string around your body just under your boobs, the length of that string is the number portion of your bra size, usually between 30 and 40. The letter refers to the cup size, starting with A and going up to DD (though some brands size up to H).

In addition to finding something that fits well and feels good, there are different types of bras for different boob needs. Your boobs will be featured in a range of fashion situations from T-shirts and tank tops to strapless or backless dresses. Your boobs could find themselves bouncing around during gym period or soccer practice, dancing or running around town. If you have a bra need, you can definitely find whatever you're looking for. Here is a run-down on some of the more common types.

TRAINING BRAS
Your first bra will probably be the oddly named "training" bra. They are small and stretchy and designed for breasts that are just starting to bud.

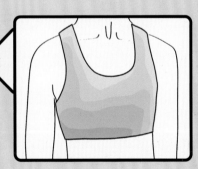

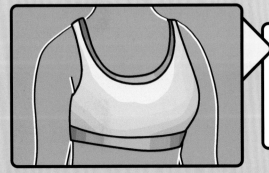

SPORTS BRAS
Jiggly boobs can be painful. Tight but stretchy, sports bras give strong support and are designed for you to sweat in.

MORE BRAS

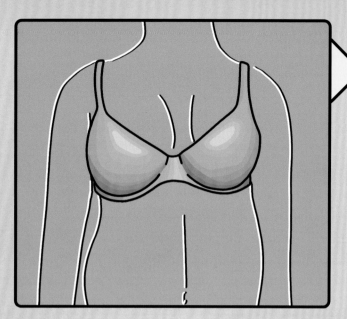

CLASSIC BRA
Bras come with or without underwire. Some girls with larger, heavier breasts like the support of an underwire bra. If your boobs are more wide-set or on the smaller side, an underwire can feel uncomfortable.

STRAPLESS BRA
Strapless bras or bandeaus make it possible to keep your shoulders bare and your breasts supported.

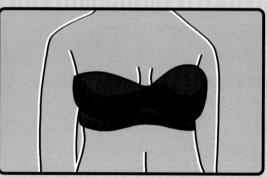

STICK-ON BRAS
Remember how much you loved stickers when you were a little kid? Stick-on bras are stickers for your boobs! If you're wearing something open in the back or super revealing, just stick these onto your breasts one at a time and then hook them together in front. Rock whatever you're wearing.

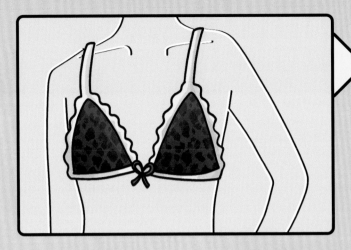

BRALETTES
Bralettes have no cups, no wires, and no padding—they are just barely a bra—but give stylish, comfortable coverage for people who are good with minimal support.

BUILT-IN BRAS Lots of tank tops, camisoles, and swimsuits come with built-in bras. An extra layer of fabric has elastic along the bottom for a little support, and some of them have removable padding too.

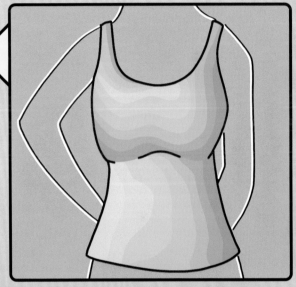

STRAP-TASTIC!
On most bras, you can adjust the length of your straps for comfort (or to see how high you can hoist your boobs up!)

Kidding.

Most bras have straps that go straight back over each shoulder. When I first started wearing a bra, I would be mortified if my bra strap peeked out from my clothing. I hadn't yet discovered all the strap (and strapless) possibilities. Racer-back bras have straps that are pulled into an X-shape in the back. Convertible straps unhook or clasp together in the back so you can wear them either way.

Moving on DOWN

"Hi."

VAGINA!

You should make a point of getting to know all your girl parts. People have a hard time saying "vagina," so let's start right there. VAGINA. Your vagina is basically a muscular tube that extends from inside of you, at your cervix, out to your vulva. There's a whole lot of other anatomy going on, and it is an excellent idea to get to know your body.

AND ONE MORE THING ABOUT THE VAGINA...

People mistakenly think of the vagina as being an open hole, but it's more like an enclosed pouch. That's the reason tampons don't disappear. They can only go in so far. Also, the walls of your vagina touch unless there is something inserted into you, like a tampon or a finger.

It is totally normal for the vagina to feel bumpy. And sometimes it may feel itchy. If your notice that it smells or feels different or uncomfortable, talk to your doctor. You may have a yeast infection. Those are very common and easy to treat.

CLITORIS Only a tiny tip of your clitoris is visible from the outside. The clitoris goes deep inside of you and contains 8,000 nerve endings, which make it very sensitive. It is covered and protected by the clitoral hood.

URETHRA This is a tiny opening that's really hard to see, but you'll know where it is because it is where urine comes out.

VULVA Often mistaken for the vagina, the vulva is the outside end of the vagina and includes the inner and outer lips .

The color of everything in the vulva region will vary depending on your skin tone.

VAGINA

VESTIBULE The vestibule is like a lobby or entryway to your vagina.

LABIA MAJORA OR OUTER LIPS Pubic hair grows on these outer, visible lips whose job is to protect the sensitive inner parts.

ANUS The opening where solid waste (poop!) leaves the body.

LABIA MINOR OR INNER LIPS The inner lips have oil glands and keep you lubricated. When you feel wet inside, that's coming from the labia minor. They come in many different shapes and sizes and are often uneven. Yours will most likely look different from this illustration.

The SKIN You're In

From your huge, hobbit feet to the breakout on your forehead, no part of your body is untouched by puberty. While hips and boobs can be really exciting, I'm not gonna lie. There's nothing fun about zits. And most of us—a whopping 80 percent—will have to deal with acne during puberty.

ZITS AND OTHER INDIGNITIES

As with everything else at the carnival that is puberty, hormones are behind your wonky skin situation. Here's what's going on: The pores (hair follicles) in your skin contain *sebaceous glands*, also called oil glands. These glands make up sebum, which is the oil that lubricates your hair and skin so they look and feel good. Most of the time, your body makes just enough sebum to keep your skin healthy and working properly. But during puberty, the hormonal changes overstimulate the oil glands. So instead of looking dewy and smooth, you wind up all shiny and bumpy.

When there is too much sebum, your pores get clogged with dead skin cells. Bacteria can get trapped inside those clogged pores. That's when the fun begins! The next thing you know, swelling, redness, whiteheads (clogged, closed pores), blackheads (open clogged pores), and pimples (clogged pores with bacteria mixed in) are throwing a party on your face. Did you ever get a large, painful zit with a pus-filled center? That's your body's reaction to a bacterial infection. It's gross and miserable, BUT it does come to an end. In the meantime, there are some things you can do to make it less horrible.

YOUR SKINCARE SURVIVAL GUIDE

It seems so obvious, but the best thing you can do is to keep your face clean. Use facial cleanser or facial soap (not just any old soap or body wash) and water twice a day to wash away dirt. If you have breakouts or oily skin, look for a cleanser with salicylic acid or benzoyl peroxide. You can also apply creams containing these ingredients directly on the zits. Do not touch your pimples except for the one or two times a day when you are applying zit cream. In case of really, really bad breakouts, you can try a gel that contains adapalene. Be careful that you don't overuse any of these products, because they can be really drying.

A little dab of this and a tiny drop of that . . .

If your zits look more like giant bumps or cysts, you should probably go to a dermatologist (a skin doctor). A doctor might prescribe a heavy-duty acne cream or even an antibiotic to kill the bacteria causing the pimples. I have friends who went on antibiotics and it definitely helped.

Drink lots of water, eliminate soda, and limit sugar and fats. Some people think that eating orange and yellow fruits and vegetables (like carrots, sweet potatoes, and apricots) can help. Foods rich in zinc, such as pumpkin seeds and quinoa, are also supposed to be good for your skin. The truth is the thing that makes the biggest difference of all is time. Once your hormones start to calm down, your oil glands will follow, and your gorgeous glow will return.

HIDING IN PLAIN SIGHT

There are tons of YouTube and TikTok tutorials on how to cover zits with green concealer or powder or other tricks. And they can be very effective if you are going somewhere special and don't want an unsightly headlight ruining your good time. But avoid heavy concealers and try to minimize the amount of touching in general since you will be doing further damage by irritating skin and introducing more bacteria.

Hair, hair, EVERYWHERE!

In addition to sprouting up and out during puberty, you will grow hair—lots of it—in new and exciting places. Some girls go through puberty and still look pretty hairless. Others might find their coarse, dark arm hairs work even better than a sweater. Hair growth—from pubic hair to underarm hair to everywhere else—varies wildly from body to body.

pubic hair

Sometime between the ages of 7 and 13 (possibly earlier or later), you will begin to notice pubic hair. Pubes are usually curly and darker than the hair on your head. You may wind up with a light sprinkling of hair, or a full-on bush that even trails up to your bellybutton and down to your vulva. It can spill out towards your thighs as well. It varies a lot girl to girl. For every girl, the pubes function like eyebrows for your vulva. They are there to keep dirt and bacteria out. It can feel really weird at first to see hair down there. But eventually it will feel normal, just like all your other new puberty accessories.

UNDERARM HAIR

Speaking of smooth, bald areas being overtaken by hair, your underarms will soon be home to a little forest as well. Sometime between the ages of 9 and 13, you will notice a silky hair or 2 or 200. By this time, you will have already sprouted boobs and pubes, so it may not seem like the biggest deal in the world. Or maybe you will want to throw out all your tank tops. A lot of grown women shave their underarm hair, which makes those little tufts of fluff seem really strange. But they're not.

I DON'T WANT HAIR *THERE!*

We are born with tiny, fine, nearly invisible hairs all over our body. When we hit puberty, many of those hairs grow thicker and darker. Your arms and legs may start to look furry. You could grow a Frida Kahlo mustache. Your two eyebrows may stretch into one long eyebrow. You could have hair anywhere and everywhere from your toes to your chinny chin chin. Trust me.

The weird, random hair growth slows down when your hormones normalize, when you are out the other end of puberty. If you love your new fur coat, you go girl! I had a friend on the track team in my school who was always wearing shorts and never shaved anything. She rocked her ankle-to-hip hairy legs, bushy armpits, the works. She really proved that everything looks good if you wear it with confidence. If you prefer a smoother look, check out page 50 for your best hair removal options.

THE RAZOR AND THE HAIR

First off, if you are comfortable with your body hair, there is not a reason in the world to get rid of it. Braid it, flaunt it, leave it be. If you want to be smooth and shiny, there are lots of ways to get there, some temporary, some permanent. Some girls groom in the warmer months and opt for insulation when it's cold out and they're covered up. Use the following chart to help figure out what's right for you.

Hair REMOVAL Techniques

METHOD	HOW IT WORKS	BEST FOR	PAIN FACTOR
SHAVING	Lather area with soap or shaving cream. Holding the razor right next to your skin, move in the direction of hair growth.	Legs, underarms, pubic hair (trim pubic hair first)	Painless unless you cut yourself (be careful!)
WAXING	Wax or a wax strip is applied to skin, smoothed on, and then pulled off against the direction of hair growth.	Legs, arms, armpits, face, bikini line	Like ripping off lots of Band-Aids pain. Hurts more in areas with more nerve endings like the bikini line and above the lip.
DEPILATORIES	Spread cream on unwanted hair, wait for chemicals to work, and then magically rinse clean.	Legs, arms, armpits, face, bikini line	Totally painless but test to make sure your skin does not react to it.
ELECTROLYSIS	A technician inserts a tiny probe into the hair follicle and electrocutes it so that it will stop producing hair.	Small areas like the face since hairs are removed one at a time.	Electric charge in hair follicle = OUCH
LASER HAIR REMOVAL	A technician uses a laser to damage the hair follicle.	Legs, arms, armpits, face, bikini line	Not as painful as electrolysis but you are still burning hair follicles
TRIMMING	Use small scissors to carefully trim unwanted hair	Armpits, bikini line	Painless
TWEEZING	Use a tweezer to pluck individual hairs	Eyebrows, bikini, chin	Quick ouch

EXPENSE	MAINTENANCE	PROS, CONS, NOTES
Disposable razors are inexpensive. Reusable razors are pricier but you only have to buy new blades.	Grows in as stubble. Can last from days to weeks	Super easy and convenient. Can cause ingrown hairs.
Pricey if you go to a salon to have it done. You can also purchase wax strips at a most drugstores.	Can last for weeks or even a month or more.	It becomes less painful and the hair will start to grow in thinner. Can cause ingrown hairs.
Inexpensive depending on brand.	Can last for a few days to a few weeks.	Chemicals meant to burn off hair can also burn your skin, so be careful.
You must go to a technician for this and it's expensive.	It's permanent.	Most technicians will numb the area beforehand.
Very expensive because you need to go to a technician	If done repeatedly, it is permanent.	Works best on people with darker hair and lighter skin because the contrast allows the hair to absorb the heat.
Inexpensive	Requires regular maintenance	Some people have light enough growth that the occasional trim will do the trick.
Inexpensive	Hair will grow back	Fine for a small area or an odd hair or two.

Something SMELLS Funny

What looks like armpit hair to you looks like a warm, cozy home to bacteria. When you were a little kid running around the playground, you could get overheated and sweaty and still smell like sugar and spice. Those days are over. Between your overactive sweat glands and your hairy armpits, you smell like your sweaty uncle after a game of one-on-one.

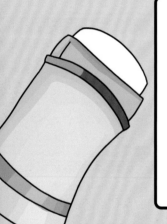

It's time to meet deodorant. Put a little on each armpit in the morning. If you play sports after school, take one in your backpack for some post-practice reinforcement. Be sure to use deodorant, not antiperspirant. Antiperspirant stops you from sweating, and sweating is healthy and cool and something you should definitely do. Wash your pits with soap and water in the shower.

IT'S OK TO SMELL HUMAN!

You may notice new smells coming from your panty region. You've got hair and bacteria down there now too. There are a lot of products on the shelves and ads designed to make you think you should smell like something other than you—wipes, sprays, and douches. Your vagina maintains a perfect and delicate balance on its own. You can clean yourself in the bath or shower with water. Do not wipe, spray, or insert anything scented into your vagina or you could upset that natural balance. You could get itchy or stingy, and that is way worse than smelling like a human being.

Am I WEIRD???

Sometimes, even stuff that is perfectly normal seems very, VERY odd. Puberty can feel like a freak show. Rest assured, there's nothing wrong with you, and the freaky stuff will come to an end.

ONE OF MY BREASTS IS WAY BIGGER THAN THE OTHER!

It's very common for one boob to develop earlier or faster than the other. They should mostly even out, but don't be alarmed if they are not identical twins. About 25 percent of fully grown women have breasts that are not quite the same in terms of size and shape.

I HAVE HAIR GROWING ON MY NIPPLES.

The same supercharged hormones that cause you to grow pubic hair and turn up the volume on your body hair can also darken and thicken the fine, invisible hairs around your nipples. Yeah, a nipple 'stache is not the prettiest side effect of puberty. You can safely tweeze them and know that once your hormone levels even out you won't look like the grandpa at the swimming pool with the wiry hairs in weird places.

UM, I SEEM TO HAVE A BEARD.

At some point in your life, you'll be psyched about the estrogen effect of thicker hair on your head. Right now, the supersizing of invisible peach fuzz is probably grossing you out. A boy I liked in high school tried to brush a chin hair off of me, thinking it must be an eyelash. I'll never forget the look on his face when he realized it was attached. You can pluck stray hairs with a tweezer. Lots of people wax their lady mustaches. If it's really bad and bothering you, electrolysis or laser treatments are an option.

I'm a mutant!

MY FACE TOTALLY CHANGED.

It's normal for girls' faces to grow longer and more angular during puberty. Some girls start out with large features that they grow into. I had a truly massive forehead when I was a kid—it had its own highlighting in selfies! But after puberty, the rest of my face seemed to catch up to it. I have a friend whose straight nose grew a pronounced bump when she went through puberty. When you run into grown-ups you haven't seen in awhile, there's a reason they may say, "I didn't recognize you!"

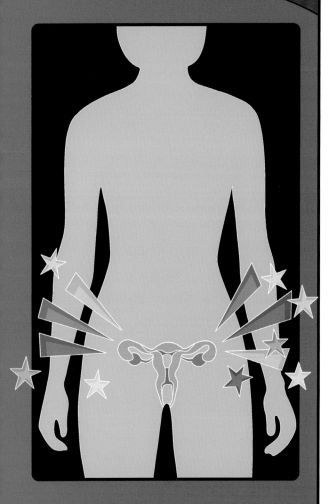

Getting your first period is a major focus of girlhood—not just among your friends but in books and movies too. It's the milestone that every girl in the world dreams about, dreads, and eventually shares. I got my period in the middle of my 15th birthday party. Safe to say it was NOT my favorite birthday present. I actually didn't know it was my period at first and had to call my mom into the bathroom to confirm. Your special visitor can arrive any time between the ages of 8 and 16. And it can take six months to a year or more before you are on a regular monthly schedule.

WHAT EXACTLY IS GOING ON?

The menstrual cycle happens over the course of about a month, though it could take anywhere from 21 to 35 days that roll out roughly like this:

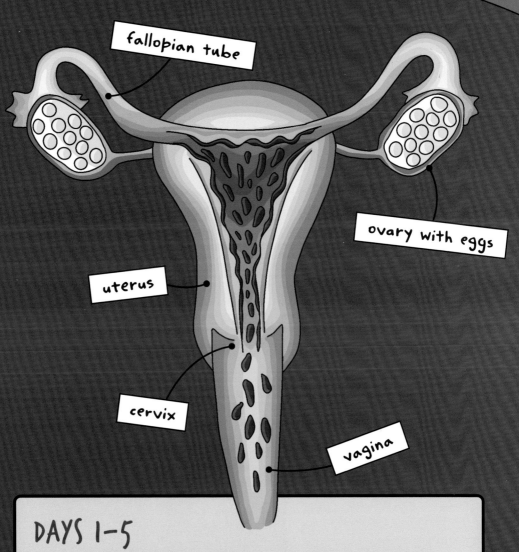

fallopian tube

ovary with eggs

uterus

cervix

vagina

DAYS 1-5

The part you think of as your period, the **menses** phase, happens during the first five days of the cycle. "That time of the month" is when you shed the lining of your uterus. If you are not pregnant, the skin cells and blood cells leave your body through your vagina, which is a technical way of saying you bleed—usually for three to five days. Blood doesn't come gushing out of you. It flows or seeps out. The flow starts out heavier, then gets lighter until it stops.

AND THEN . . .

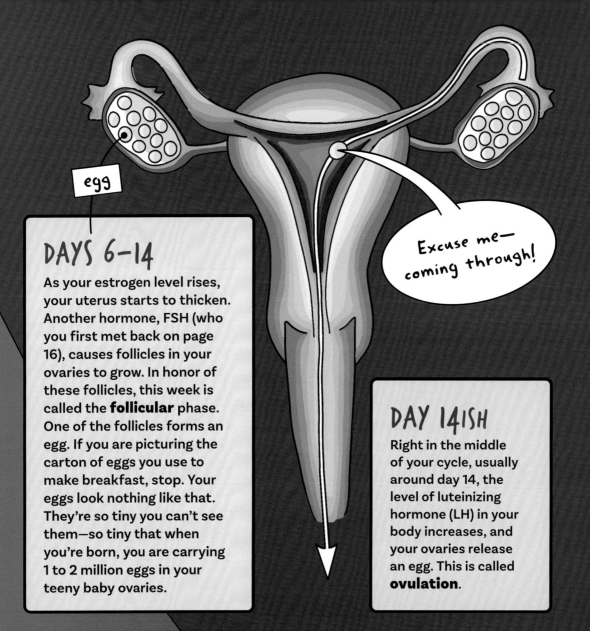

egg

Excuse me— coming through!

DAYS 6-14

As your estrogen level rises, your uterus starts to thicken. Another hormone, FSH (who you first met back on page 16), causes follicles in your ovaries to grow. In honor of these follicles, this week is called the **follicular** phase. One of the follicles forms an egg. If you are picturing the carton of eggs you use to make breakfast, stop. Your eggs look nothing like that. They're so tiny you can't see them—so tiny that when you're born, you are carrying 1 to 2 million eggs in your teeny baby ovaries.

DAY 14ISH

Right in the middle of your cycle, usually around day 14, the level of luteinizing hormone (LH) in your body increases, and your ovaries release an egg. This is called **ovulation**.

DAYS 15-28 OR THEREABOUTS

The rest of your cycle, about two weeks, is the **luteal** phase. This describes the egg's wild ride from the ovary through your fallopian tubes and into the uterus. Progesterone joins the hormone party now. If this month's egg is not fertilized by sperm, then estrogen and progesterone levels drop. Your uterus prepares to shed its lining. And the cycle starts all over again.

THE POLITICS OF PERIODS

Though boys go through puberty, get hairy, and their voices change, there is not an equivalent milestone to the period. They don't have shark week or a visit from Aunt Flo every month for the next 30 to 40 years of their lives. And they don't have to deal with the monthly expense of buying products to make sure they don't bleed all over the place. Some schools and businesses recognize this imbalance and provide free period products, but mostly we're on our own. As a menstruating woman, you may be noticing for the first time that we pay an actual price for being a girl.

OH, HORMONES...

As you can see from this breakdown of the roller-coaster ride that is your menstrual cycle, the levels of many different hormones in your body are going up and down over the course of the month. Feeling "hormonal" is very real! For some girls that might mean you get particular food cravings right before your period. I have such serious chocolate and salty food cravings I can predict the arrival of my period based on chip bags and candy bar wrappers. Some girls get headaches or cramps. Some feel sad for no real reason, and others feel angry. You may feel all of these things. It's normal. It's hormones.

Some girls use a period tracking app so they can better anticipate when they'll get their period or when they might feel moody. If you're feeling really angry or sad, it can be helpful to know that there's a hormonal reason, and the intense feelings will pass.

Menstrual SYMPTOMS

Sometimes your menstrual cycle runs smoothly, like a train making all its stops at the right time, no fuss. And sometimes, the ride can get bumpy.

In fifth grade, when the school nurse rolled out a huge, old dusty TV and played a video about puberty, the voice-over explained that although we would bleed during our periods, it wouldn't hurt. That wasn't exactly true.

SURPRISE! (CRAMPS)

When my periods became more regular, I started to realize that I would get these weird stomachaches every month. They weren't really painful, just annoying.

Stomachaches that coincide with the beginning of your period are called menstrual or period cramps. Mine feel like a dull ache in my lower belly and usually ease up after a few days. Some people experience sharper pain. Some of my friends have cramps during their entire period, while others don't experience period cramps at all.

If your cramps get really uncomfortable, try taking a warm bath, putting a hot water bottle or heating pad on your belly, or taking some ibuprofen. If your period cramps *really* hurt, or if you feel cramping outside of your monthly cycle, you should let your doctor know.

P.S. PMS

In addition to feeling crampy, my emotions run a bit hot a few days before my period. My temper becomes shorter, and I get tired. Sometimes, I'll watch a sad TikTok video about a puppy and just start crying. These emotional changes in energy are called premenstrual syndrome (PMS). Some people also get bloated as a side effect and can put on a few pounds of (temporary) water weight.

Who Has PMS?

PMS has a pretty bad rap. Some men, even male doctors, can be dismissive about it, as if it's a made-up condition. Others like to shame women who are angry or sad by accusing them of having PMS. My brother loved to taunt me during arguments by saying, "Ooh, you must be on your period." PMS is real. And it is never OK for someone who doesn't menstruate to tell you what you must be feeling.

IF YOU FEEL SOMETHING, SAY SOMETHING.

Listen to your changing body. Discomfort before and during your period is perfectly normal. Moodiness and headaches are normal too—and should pass when your period ends. Severe pain and alarming mood swings—symptoms that drastically interfere with your life—might require some help. Discuss any concerns you have with a doctor, therapist, or trusted adult.

THAT'S DEFINITELY KETCHUP

The very first time I got my period, I was running late to school and shoved one of my sister's pads into my underpants. It may not have been in exactly the right spot. Later on, at lunchtime in the cafeteria, I stood up to put my tray away and there was period blood on my seat! The boy sitting next to me pointed down and asked, "What is that?" Luckily, I was wearing black pants. And luckily, my friend (who knew I had just gotten my period) said, "Ooh you sat on ketchup," took a napkin, and wiped it up.

It takes awhile to figure out which product works best for you, what size you'll need at different points in your cycle, and even how often you need to change. The flow is *usually* heavier for the first one to three days and then gets lighter each day. Some girls need "super-plus" tampons or maxi pads every single day, and others can get by with normal or even slender absorbency. You will have to experiment and figure out what makes you feel comfortable and secure. And that winning formula may change from cycle to cycle.

FEMININE HYGIENE 101

Most girls start out using pads and then transition to tampons. But there are lots of feminine hygiene options, and you'll need to figure out what works for you.

Tampons are inserted into your vagina where they absorb the blood. Applicator-free tampons are more compact and portable and more eco-friendly. They can also be a bit trickier to insert. Tampons come in different sizes for light, normal, and heavier flow. You are using the right size if your tampon is full but not leaking after four hours. Whichever type you use, tampons need to be replaced every four to eight hours for the duration of your period.

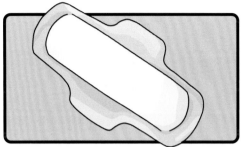

Pads stick to your underpants and absorb the blood. They come in different thicknesses for heavy and light days and also need to be changed every four to eight hours.

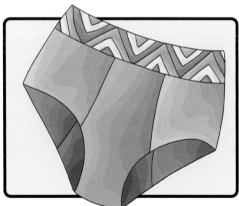

Period underwear are a newish product designed to cut down on waste. Some girls, with a lighter flow, wear them with no other products, in which case they need to be rinsed out at the end of the day, then thrown into the wash. Other girls wear them as an extra layer of protection if they're worried about leaking through a pad or tampon. And some girls opt for period pants at the end of their period when their flow is lightest.

Menstrual cups are cone-shaped and made of soft silicone or rubber. They are inserted into the vagina where they hold the menstrual blood. After 10 to 12 hours, the cup is pulled out, rinsed, and replaced. At the end of your period, the cup is sterilized for the next month. A menstrual cup can last for years.

Tampon DIY

When I got my period, my mom handed me a box of tampons and told me to read the instructions. That didn't go so smoothly, so I'm going to break it down as simply as possible for you.

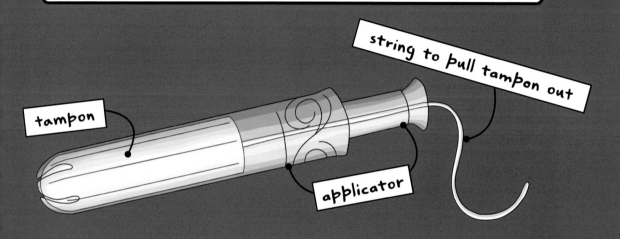

string to pull tampon out

tampon

applicator

In the US, most tampons come with a cardboard or plastic applicator. The actual tampon is white and cottony and has a string inside. The tampon is the only part that stays in your body. The applicator has an outer barrel and an inner tube that fits inside the barrel and pushes the tampon out. Note: If you are using an applicator-less tampon, you will need to use your fingers to get the tampon into the correct position.

It may take a few tries to get the hang of it. It took me way more than a few tries. I had to wear pads for my first three or four periods because I thought tampons were really uncomfortable. And then my family took a trip to the beach and I really wanted to go swimming. So I kept trying and trying and finally figured out the right angle.

1. Sit on the toilet, knees apart. Hold the middle of the tampon in between your thumb and middle finger.

2. Use the wider tip of the tampon to nudge open the folds of skin on your vagina. Gently slide the entire barrel inside. Do not aim straight up (that will hurt). Instead, insert the applicator at an angle. Remember when you studied angles in school? Imagine a 45-degree angle. That should be about the angle of tampon entry, aiming toward your back.

If it hurts, it's not going in right. Re-angle until it slides in comfortably. Once you find the comfortable angle, keep pushing until the full barrel (the thick part of the tampon) is inside of you.

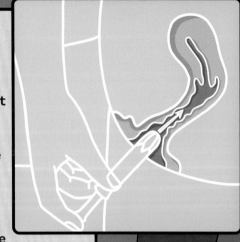

3. Now, using your index finger on the end of the thinner tube, push the thinner tube in all the way. This will force the tampon out of the barrel and deeper into your vagina.

4. Once the barrel is empty and the tampon is nestled inside your vagina, slide the applicator out. The string that's attached to the tampon should be visible, conveniently hanging out of your vagina. (It gets less freaky with time.)

5. In about four hours, when your tampon is filled with blood, you will tug the handy string to pull it out. Then repeat these steps with a shiny new tampon. For now, place the applicator inside its wrapper (or wrap in toilet paper) and toss in a trash bin. Your used tampon should not be flushed either—it could clog your toilet. Wrap it up in toilet paper and toss it in the trash.

Am I WEIRD???

MY PERIOD BLOOD IS MORE BROWN THAN RED.

That is the glorious result of oxidation, which means that your period blood had time to mix with oxygen and turn brown. Basically, it's some old blood! This happens a lot at the beginning and end of a period, when your flow is a bit slower.

MY PERIOD COMES AND GOES.

For the first few years after your first period, your cycle will probably be really irregular. Skipping many months or even up to a year between your first and second periods is totally normal. Some girls are irregular for years. Stress, low body weight, overexercising, undereating, and certain medications can cause irregular periods.

I GET A MIGRAINE EVERY MONTH.

Hormone headaches are so common there's a name for them. If you have a throbbing headache along with sensitivity to light, smells, or sound within a few days of getting your period, this is due to hormones. Migraines can last for a few hours and up to a few days. Talk to your doctor about treatments if they become a serious problem.

I POOP MORE WHEN I HAVE MY PERIOD.

Period poops are a thing. The same hormones that help the muscles in your uterus relax and shed its lining have a similar effect on your bowels. For many girls, that means more poop and even diarrhea. For some, it can cause constipation. It's very common to experience issues with your bowels around your period.

PART 2

CHANGES ON THE INSIDE

The same hormones that transform your body during puberty make things more . . . complicated in your brain. Part 1 focused mostly on external, or outside, changes. Your skin, your boobs, your hair, hair everywhere. But you're not only growing physically–you're also doing A LOT of growing mentally and emotionally. Your grown-up body comes with grown-up feelings.

Just wait until your moods swing so hard and fast that you go from laughing your head off with your friends to wishing they would go far, far away from you. Wait until your first real-person crush or the first pubescent fight with your parents. I argued with my parents about ridiculous things, from letting me have back-to-back sleepovers to serving salad without dressing. Even just a few years out the other side, I can tell you that nothing is as big and bad as it seems at the time. I remember mourning One Direction's breakup like I knew them personally. I was totally irrational. Why oh why do we feel so many things in so little time? That's puberty, brought to you by hormones gone wild. I'll tell you all about it–and I promise you'll make it through too!

Feeling... SEXUAL?

One of the weirdest, most surprising, and fun changes during puberty involves the development of sexual feelings. The scientific explanation for this is because increases in the hormones estrogen, testosterone, and progesterone that trigger physical changes in your body also influence sexual desire and attraction. So what does this actually mean?

Well, you know that dorky kid who always dips his fries in applesauce at lunch? You might start noticing that— wait—he's actually kinda cute? Or the girl who always galloped around the yard at recess, pretending to be a horse? All of a sudden you begin to notice she smells like ...fresh laundry and lemons.

You might blush and feel warm and fluttery when a certain boy or girl looks at you a certain way. You may notice someone's long eyelashes or wavy hair and feel something almost waking up inside you. However you experience it, you're likely to start responding to other people in a different way. For the first time in your life, you are experiencing romantic and sexual feelings. This could range from finding people cute or wanting to spend all your time with them to dreaming about them, and wanting to kiss them. Eventually, maybe even something more.

This might start out with an innocent crush on some fictional character (one of my buddies in middle school had a massive crush on Padme from *Star Wars*). Or maybe you find yourself developing feelings for your best friend (totally not speaking from experience on this one). The point is, girls going through puberty notice sexual feelings in a variety of ways. Some girls in my class were definitely flirting by fourth grade. Others don't experience their first "awakening" until high school. No rush. You'll know it when you feel it.

DO YOU LIKE, LIKE ME?

Attraction can hit you fast, like a light switch turning on, or more gradually. You know how in the movies you see characters doing outrageous things, like jumping on a table and singing, when they fall for someone? In real life, we may do awkward, embarrassing things too. You might find yourself blushing like crazy or stammering all over the place when you're around someone you have feelings for. In fifth grade, one of my friends used to make me chase down the boy she liked at recess to give him a note asking whether he liked her. In seventh grade, I had a serious crush on a boy on my ultimate frisbee team. I saw him a lot at practice and did absolutely nothing about it. Keeping our crushes to ourselves is also normal.

THE CONTINUUM OF ATTRACTION

The wide variety of ways to experience sexual feelings doesn't only apply to the intensity of feelings. There may also be a range of people for whom you feel attraction. Around puberty is usually the time you start to figure out whether you like boys, girls, both, or neither. Girls can like boys, or girls and boys, or just girls.

Sometimes girls don't experience sexual feelings at all. Girls can also prefer one gender but be open to both. Here's the important part: **There is no right answer when it comes to love**. Everyone's relationships and experiences are important, whether they are gay, straight, bisexual, pansexual, asexual, or something else. What matters is allowing yourself to feel what you feel, and respect that other people may have different experiences from you.

CRUSH OR FRIENDSHIP?

Knowing the difference between platonic (or friend) feelings and crushes can be tricky. When your hormones are wacky and the most important relationships in your life have been platonic up to this point, it can be hard to know whether your feelings for someone are strong friend feelings or romantic feelings. This seems especially hard when your confused feelings are for someone of the same gender. Take your time, and don't stress out about it. There's absolutely no rush to get a boyfriend or girlfriend right now. Crushes can be short-lived. What's most important is understanding and accepting yourself.

While most girls you know probably like boys, a growing percentage of people identify as LGBTQ+. Coming to terms with your identity if you're not straight can be nerve-racking. While it is completely normal to have same-sex feelings, there are still many people who don't accept or understand the continuum of attraction. Hiding your feelings out of fear can be really hard. That being said, there are way more people out there who will love and accept you no matter who you love.

THE ABCs OF LBGTQ

You've likely heard the words "gay" and "straight" by now, but let's break it down a little further.

LGBTQ+ refers to the broader community of queer people. It stands for Lesbian, Gay, Bisexual, Transgender, and Queer, with a plus sign to indicate further gender identities and sexualities.

LESBIAN: Girls who are romantically, emotionally, or sexually attracted to other girls.

GAY: Boys who are romantically, emotionally, or sexually attracted to other boys.

BISEXUAL: A person attracted to more than one gender.

TRANSGENDER: Someone who doesn't identify with the sex they were assigned at birth.

QUEER: Anyone who is not straight. This used to be seen as an offensive word but has recently been taken back by the LGBTQ+ community.

Just as there's no rush to get a boyfriend all of a sudden, there's also no rush to come out as gay or bisexual if you're not sure or ready. It can depend a lot on the people around you and how accepting they are. I came out as bisexual in the middle of high school. I had classmates who came out in middle school. And I know people in college who still haven't come out to their families. It doesn't matter when you come out. What matters is that you know there is absolutely nothing wrong with you for feeling attracted to other girls if you do.

+ ASEXUALITY

Not everyone experiences sexual feelings during puberty. Some people don't mature sexually until much later than others. However, for some people, these feelings never really arrive. Part of the plus in the LGBTQ+ community includes those who are asexual–people who have a complete or partial lack of sexual feelings. I've had asexual friends who feel absolutely zero attraction to other people and some who very rarely feel sexual attraction. It all depends on the person and, once more, it is nothing to be ashamed of, even if those around you all report having sexual feelings.

The Why of WETNESS

Before I went through puberty, I knew that one day I would wake up and see blood and know I had my period. I didn't know I might see other things going on in my underpants. Before you get your period, you may start to notice discharge—a thin clear or whitish fluid—in the lining of your underwear. This is completely normal and actually the stuff that keeps your vagina clean and free from infection.

But wait, there's more! There's another type of discharge or wetness called arousal fluid. When you start having sexual thoughts or urges, that feeling is called "arousal." When you are "aroused," there is increased blood flow to your genitals, causing fluid to pass through your vaginal walls and make your vaginal tissue wet. Arousal fluid looks a lot like vaginal discharge, but it tends to be clear and more slippery.

This is all a very technical way of saying that when you start having sexual feelings, you're also going to start experiencing wetness from your vagina.

Everything OK sweetie? You've been in there a long time.

MASTURBATION NATION

Sexual feelings introduce sensations you've never had before. And it's totally normal to explore those feelings, to touch yourself and see what feels good where. There's a word for this: masturbation. Supercool term right? It doesn't at all sound like some weird way to cook a chicken.

So what is masturbation? Basically, it's the act of pleasuring yourself, usually by touching or rubbing your genitals. I'm not about to give a how-to on masturbating because this isn't that kind of book. But you should know that exploring your body and masturbating is a completely healthy, natural, and private activity.

Both the girl who has no interest in masturbating and the girl who masturbates on the regular are completely valid, healthy people. I know girls who never even considered masturbation until college, and I know girls who were masturbating regularly as early as middle school. Some people have zero interest in masturbating. What matters most is that you do what makes you feel comfortable, explore at your own pace, and don't feel ashamed about getting to know your body.

MOODS & Mood Swings

The new feelings you'll experience during puberty aren't all warm and fuzzy and fluttery. Estrogen, testosterone, and progesterone, the hormones that trigger physical changes and sexual feelings, also impact your moods in a big way. The best way I can describe it is like you've been strapped into a never-ending roller coaster. You're going up and up for a while, and it's pretty chill, and then all of a sudden you're plummeting to the ground, but then oh, wait, you're heading up again. We call these mood swings.

Going from happy to sad to ticked off in the space of a few hours is a special kind of emotional whiplash. To complicate things a little further, in the days leading up to your period, your estrogen fluctuates, and you can feel even moodier. I know, I know, this sounds a little bleak. But I promise you, no matter how confused, mad, sad, or annoyed you may feel, these feelings are temporary. You're going to swing right back into equilibrium soon enough.

HULKING Out

When we were
in middle
school, my
brother started
calling me "The
Hulk." Not because
I could turn green
and bulk up to the point
where my clothes would
shred, but because I had a
tendency to get very angry very quickly.
I would (in my family's words) "hulk out" at the smallest things:
my brother accidentally jostling me on the way out of the car, my
parents asking me to do the dishes when I was clearly in the middle
of a TV episode, even someone carrying a conversation on just a
little too long. In a lot of ways, I did feel a bit like a mild-mannered
scientist who suddenly had very little control over my anger. I didn't
want to be mad, but it seemed like the whole world had reorganized
to infuriate me. Of course, this wasn't the case. I was just dealing
with a lot of new adult emotions and a brain not developed and
experienced enough to process them, so it reverted to something it
knew well: anger.

There's a reason "angry teens" are a cliché—teens are angry! The parts of the brain that control reasoning and impulses are not nearly developed enough in teenagers to cope with the intense feelings brought on by the hormones flooding your body. It's like you've been plunked into the driver's seat in a moving car, but you don't know how to drive yet. Feeling angry is not unique to teenagers. Struggling to control that anger is.

ANGER MANAGEMENT FOR TEENS

So what can you do with all that anger? A few things:

Take a break. If you find yourself getting angry, walk away. Take a walk or go for a run or bike around the block or step into another room for a few minutes. Tell whoever you are fighting with that you need to take some space. If you can't physically leave the room, try closing your eyes and taking some slow, deep breaths in through your nose and out through your mouth.

Go to your happy place. When your temper is flaring, think about places, people, or activities that bring you joy. Remind yourself that your anger is temporary. Imagine it melting away, rolling off your body.

Pet a dog or cat. For real, petting an animal releases the feel-good chemical oxytocin and lowers blood pressure.

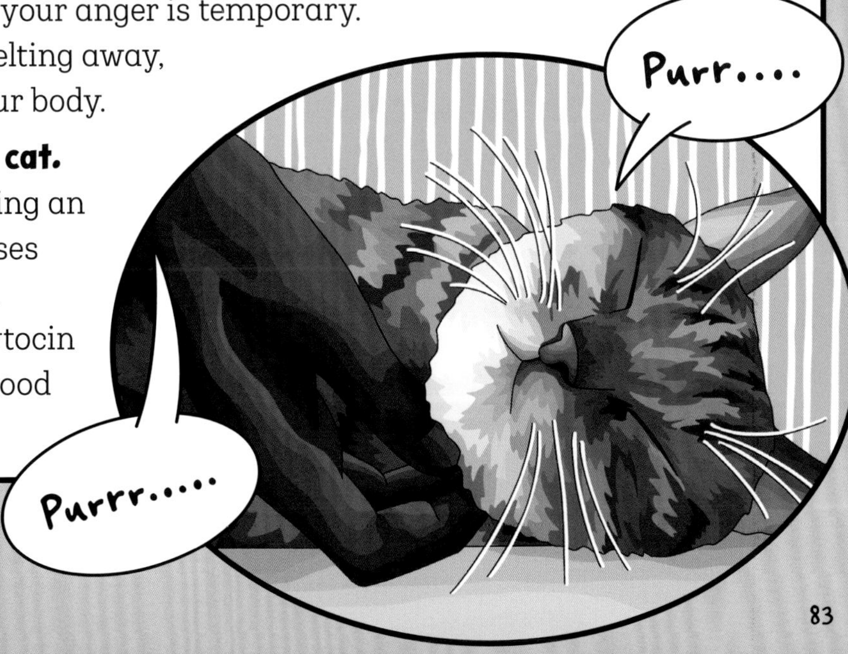

Purr....

Purrr.....

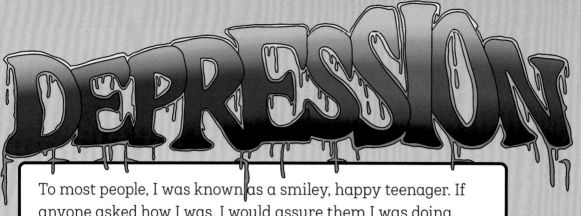

DEPRESSION

To most people, I was known as a smiley, happy teenager. If anyone asked how I was, I would assure them I was doing so well. I didn't want anyone to know that I was seriously depressed. Sounds fun right? My depression hit really hard in high school. I couldn't sleep at night and stayed in bed all day. I stopped eating as much as I should and had weekly panic attacks. Eventually, and reluctantly, with help and guidance from a therapist, I went on medication. My therapist always said, "Skills before pills." I had to learn techniques to help ease my depression as well. For many girls, the end of puberty brings an end to these intense feelings. I still rely on my skills and pills, but now I'm as happy as I appear to be.

Have you ever felt sad for no real reason, like you just can't shake the sadness? Maybe you're no longer interested in being with your friends or dancing or playing soccer. Some days you just want to hang out in bed and stream movies you've already seen. Any of these symptoms along with feeling hopeless, low-energy, or distracted might be depression. And there are lots of things that could make you feel that way. The changes you're going through, shifts in your social group, schoolwork—any and all of these things could cause depression. (Of course, serious life events like bullying or the death of a loved one would be a major cause of depression.) Unfortunately, depression is really common, especially among teenage girls. That doesn't mean it's easy.

Depression can feel all-encompassing, isolating, and scary. Depression can feel like you will never NOT be depressed, or that you are completely alone. **Neither of these is true.** The most important thing to remember is that these feelings will end. It could take hours, days, weeks, or even months. Talk to your parents or another trusted adult and definitely get help from a counselor or therapist. And trust me, you will absolutely feel better.

ANGSTing

Gone are the days when you could kick back and drink a cool glass of juice after school. Now you have homework, extracurricular activities, maybe siblings to help take care of, or even a job. Figuring out how to manage these things can be stressful.

ANXIETY

When stress feels overwhelming, you've turned the corner to anxiety land. Anxiety is a worry that lasts even after the stressful thing is no longer an issue. For me, anxiety can manifest as stomachaches or a feeling of dread in my chest. One of my friends feels nauseous

when she has anxiety. Another gets jittery and has to constantly be in motion, like a shark. My anxiety would stop me from going to parties and joining clubs in school.

Anxiety can be caused by a lot of different things. Some people have specific triggers, like social interactions or homework due dates. Some people experience anxiety about more general things, like college plans, what happens after we die, or having to speak publicly. Some people may seem to have anxiety about everyone and everything (this is called generalized anxiety).

Anxiety can be helpful, especially when you have things like a test or a soccer game coming up. A healthy level of anxiety will motivate you to study and practice and prepare. However, anxiety above this level can become harmful or even debilitating.

The best thing you can do if you're feeling anxious is to focus on the here and now. Don't think about next week or month or year. Focus on today. Is everything OK right this minute? Are you anxious about something real or imagined? I've wasted a lot of time worrying about things that might happen, such as not getting into the school I want or accidentally making a fool of myself in front of my peers. A lot of people need professional help for coping with anxiety. If you think you may be one of those people, you should definitely talk to a parent or trusted adult. A therapist can help you to build skills to manage your anxiety.

YOUR BRAIN, YOUR MOODS

Some people have a chemical imbalance in their brain that can make depression worse. If you feel like this is you, reach out to a trusted adult in your life to talk about getting a therapist. For some people, medication may be necessary too. There is absolutely no shame in getting help. I've been in therapy for years. Everyone needs to ask for help sometimes, and it's important to do so.

Feeling... HAPPY?

From the darkest days to the angriest rages to the peaks of parental irritation, there were a few reliable things that always made me feel a bit better. I'm not saying you can tie up all of these big feelings with a ribbon, but let's say your worst days can be less sucky if you:

Get outside. For better or worse, technology takes up a huge part of our lives now. Often, this means we spend a lot of time inside on our phones or computer screens, neglecting to go outside. This is a bad idea because going outside is actually... (wait for it) good for you. From walking around the block to spending the day hiking to just sitting outside soaking up some sunshine for a few minutes, exposing yourself to nature actually boosts your mood.

Exercise. Don't worry, I'm not suggesting you pump iron at the gym or anything (unless you want to, in which case, you go girl). Blast your favorite tunes and dance, skip down the street, sweat. Your body will release powerful chemicals called endorphins that create feelings of... happiness.

Rest. For the love of all that is holy, GO TO BED. Getting quality sleep on a regular schedule is so, so important during puberty. Up late binge-watching Netflix? Take a nap.

Socialize. Spending face-to-face time with people you know and like is a comfort and a distraction.

Therapy. I started seeing a therapist early on in high school for some pretty severe anxiety and depression I was having around identity and my future. Both my anxiety and depression have improved a ton. And I continue to meet with my therapist to this day. Having an unbiased person to talk to when my worry brain flares up has been so helpful. I have friends who went to therapy for a short period of time and felt it was just as effective. Sometimes we need extra help in handling our emotions.

Meditate. It sounds so weird, the idea of getting quiet and focusing on breath. But clearing your mind, deep breathing, really does reduce stress. I've found exercises like counting, say, all the objects made of wood in my room shockingly helpful. There is also the 5-4-3-2-1 technique: name 5 things you can see, 4 things you can physically feel, 3 things you can hear, 2 things you can smell, and 1 thing you can taste. These are ways to narrow your focus which is calming.

Just give yourself time to do something, anything that brings you joy.

911: TELL A GROWN-UP IF...

If you are having a really hard time falling or staying asleep, if you have thoughts of harming yourself, or if you ever feel like life is not worth living, it's really important to tell a trusted adult as soon as possible. Sometimes, depression and anxiety can feel overwhelming. But remember, you don't have to deal with any of this alone. Below are a few phone numbers you can reach out to for immediate help.

- **SUICIDE AND CRISIS LIFELINE:** Call 988.

- **CRISIS TEXTLINE:** Text CONNECT to 741741 for immediate, free, 24/7 help with anxiety.

- **THE TREVOR LIFELINE FOR LGBTQ YOUTH:** Call 1-866-488-7386.

Am I WEIRD???

SOMETIMES I THINK I LIKE GIRLS AND SOMETIMES I THINK I LIKE BOYS.

It honestly took me years to figure out that I liked both girls and boys. Just as it's normal to flip-flop in crushes on boys, it's also really easy to have crushes across genders! There's nothing wrong with liking boys one day and girls the next day. Lots of people feel an attraction to a particular person, regardless of their gender.

I HAVE MULTIPLE CRUSHES AT THE SAME TIME.

Having a crush on someone does not mean declaring loyalty to that person for the rest of your life. Crushes are wild. In sixth grade, I had crushes on three different boys at the same time. No need to choose!

THERE ARE DAYS WHEN I JUST CRY AND I'M NOT SURE WHY.

Mood swings, even intense ones, are very common when you're going through puberty. That may mean getting really sad about seemingly small things, or feeling overly emotional. And sometimes we just cry! (If these feelings don't pass, it's important to tell a trusted adult.)

I NEVER STOP FIGHTING WITH MY PARENTS.

A big part of puberty and being a teenager is about the process of separating from our parents and becoming independent adults. It's normal for you and your parents to have different ideas about what you're ready for when, and most kids going through puberty butt heads with their parents. If and when things get heated, you and your parents can practice backing off and taking time to calm down.

PART 3

THE CHANGING WORLD

As your body, mind, and emotions change, so will your place in the world. The nature of your friendships—and your friends themselves—will evolve. School will seem different. Your relationship with your parents will shift. You will start to explore the real world, and the digital world. The view is very different when you're venturing out on your own instead of riding in the back seat of your parents' car. And the people you meet will be looking at you as not quite a kid, not quite a grown-up, but as something, someone entirely new. All of these changes can be scary—but also exciting.

FRIENDSHIPS

BEST FRIENDS FOREVER!

Your friend group can be a support system, helping you through everything from late-night homework to fugly haircuts. Your friends are the people you share secrets and crushes and your favorite T-shirts with. You can FaceTime with your friends any time of day or night to talk about absolutely nothing!

Friendship isn't always sunshine and rainbows, though. When everyone you know is going through the same enormous changes at about the same time, friendship dynamics are like a giant puzzle. A thousand-piece puzzle that looked like it was coming together on the coffee table but then someone came along and knocked over the table and spilled a bottle of water on it.

SQUADS, CLIQUES, AND THE OCCASIONAL MEAN GIRL

Friend groups definitely have their perks. It's nice being in a popping group chat and having people to hang out with. Feeling popular can boost your confidence. Spending time with friends actually makes people feel better! When things go smoothly.

However, friend groups can get *messy*. I had a hometown friend group made up of my oldest childhood friends—we went to the same elementary school and middle school and kept hanging out even when we went off to different high schools. We had group chats on every app and got together almost every weekend. It felt like we would be friends forever.

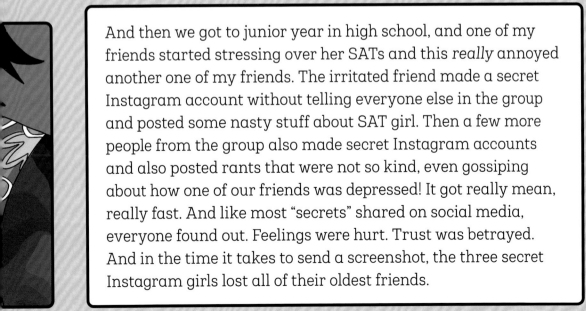

And then we got to junior year in high school, and one of my friends started stressing over her SATs and this *really* annoyed another one of my friends. The irritated friend made a secret Instagram account without telling everyone else in the group and posted some nasty stuff about SAT girl. Then a few more people from the group also made secret Instagram accounts and also posted rants that were not so kind, even gossiping about how one of our friends was depressed! It got really mean, really fast. And like most "secrets" shared on social media, everyone found out. Feelings were hurt. Trust was betrayed. And in the time it takes to send a screenshot, the three secret Instagram girls lost all of their oldest friends.

BULLYING

In eighth grade, I had a "friend" who would hang out with me after school and gossip. Normal girl stuff. Only she recorded our conversations! She then would play the recordings to all the other girls who I had bad-mouthed. Luckily, I switched schools for high school and had a chance to make new friends. There, I was in the "popular group." Until one day, without warning, I wasn't. I didn't find out why until years later. Our "queen bee" liked a boy who liked me, so she kicked me out of the friend group to punish me. I lost a group of friends for the second time and felt totally lost and lonely.

Now for the silver lining. I started hanging out with another group of girls. In my narcissistic, mean-girl, popular group phase, I thought this other group was less cool. I was so wrong. Becoming friends with those four girls was the best thing that ever happened to me. Nine years later, they are still my closest friends! And the "popular" girls who dumped me? They stopped being friends with each other right after high school.

The morals of all these friendship-gone-wrong stories?

- Don't ever say bad things about anyone else.

- Don't make judgments about who is cool. Everyone is cool in her own way.

- Friendships shift and drama happens and it seems like the biggest deal in the world at the time, but it may turn out to be exactly what you need.

- **BE KIND.**

SOMETHING OLD, SOMETHING NEW

The great thing about old friends, like the ones you used to share snacks with in preschool, is that they've known you forever. There's no explaining, and that can be really special. That long history can also become a problem when you're figuring out who you are as you transform from a little kid to a teen. Maybe you don't want to spend your time loitering at the playground or at the mall anymore. Maybe you want to try skating more and spending less time making TikToks. Just like you outgrow your stretchy striped pajamas, you can outgrow your friends. Some of my college friends remained tight with their elementary school friends. Other people made a completely fresh start when they left home.

I have friends who love their solitude, and others who need to be in a big group at all times, and some who like to be one-on-one. However you like to socialize, if you enjoy yourself and you can be yourself, it's all good.

Peer PRESSURE

When adults talk about peer pressure, they'll say things like "Don't let your friends convince you to skip school!" or "Don't go riding your bike on the wrong side of the street without a helmet just because your friends do." It may be annoying, but they are totally right. Do not listen to the classmate who tells you to throw a paper plane at your teacher's head. Definitely do not listen to the friend who dares you to drink hot sauce. Get comfortable saying, "Nah, I'm good."

Sometimes, peer pressure is more complicated than riding a bike without a helmet. Peer pressure can be unspoken too. Maybe the really cool girls at school all started wearing Air Forces. Maybe your own shoes start looking a bit lame because of it.

Going into high school I was in the popular clique. We all dyed the tips of our hair red to match and wore similar outfits to school. Even though it was not my style, I felt like I had to be just like the other girls in the group or else I would be kicked out for being different. I started painting my nails black like the other girls. I wore shirts with sassy phrases on them and way too much eyeliner. I seriously looked like a raccoon. Now, I feel better in my clothes and in my skin.

It takes courage to do your own thing and not worry about what everyone else is doing or thinking or wearing. But once you try blazing your own trail, you'll realize it's also much easier. You are smack in the middle of the process of figuring out who you are. Be someone with a strong sense of self rather than someone who follows the crowd. It may sound corny, but you will never regret following your heart instead of your friend.

Drinking, Smoking & Drugs

If you haven't already, soon, you may come across people who drink or smoke even though they are way underage.

There's a reason it's not legal to drink or smoke until you're older. There are actually a lot of reasons. First, your brain isn't fully developed. Even my brain isn't fully developed! Teenage brains are impulsive and can't anticipate repercussions. So teens have a lot of dumb ideas and don't bother thinking about where those ideas might lead. Puberty is also a really important time for your health and growth. Drinking and smoking can interrupt that growth.

There will be moments where you really feel the peer pressure. I did too! Being the only person in a room not drinking or smoking isn't easy, because it's awkward and scary being the odd one out. It's like being the only one who doesn't have red-tipped hair! But you definitely won't regret waiting until you're 21. You'll be in a much better place, physically and mentally, to make smart choices.

Dare, DOUBLE DARE?

Sometimes the process of teenagers testing boundaries looks a lot like taking stupid risks. I was pretty cautious. But I knew lots of girls who were not so worried about getting in trouble—girls who were actually thrilled by the idea of getting in trouble. For some of them, that meant shoplifting. Nail polish, bubble gum, stuff they definitely could have bought and didn't really need. For others it meant cutting classes. Some vaped. The thing is what may seem fun and cool when you're 13 could actually be dumb and possibly dangerous. So think, and then think again, before you do anything stupid, illegal, or dangerous.

Who Do You ?

Your platonic friendships are not the only relationships that change during puberty. You may be experiencing a romantic relationship for the very first time. Maybe you confessed a crush to a kid in your class. Maybe your classmate returned that crush. Maybe—just maybe—those confessions led to something different than friendship as you've known it.

KISSING IN A TREE

Early relationships can be loads of fun. I remember seeing middle school couples giggling in the boba cafes. Romantic relationships can also get weird quickly. (You know those couples who make out in the hallway like there aren't 100 people walking right by them?) When I developed feelings for my first girlfriend, I was so unsure of what I wanted that I actually broke things off for several months until I realized I was, in fact, super into her. Being part of a couple is a new experience, probably for you and your partner. It's good to figure out what you do and don't want from your relationship. Talk about it! I had a high school friend who wanted to hang out with her boyfriend every minute of every weekend, and he wanted to play basketball with his friends and go to the movies with her every now and then. That did not last long.

NOPE, NAH, NO!

Maybe you and your boyfriend hold hands in the hall at school. Maybe you and your girlfriend have kissed. Whatever you do, it's really nobody's business. The only thing that matters is your comfort (and your partner's), and your **consent**. You should never, ever do something uncomfortable to please someone else, especially when it comes to your body. And nobody should ever touch you without your permission. Not even if they beg, complain, or argue. Not even if you said yes to something ten minutes ago and changed your mind and now you're saying no. Your body is yours, and you decide what happens to it.

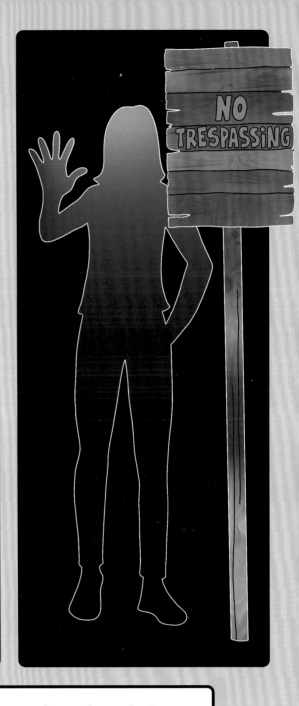

If you feel like someone ignored your boundaries or your comfort, talk about it with a parent or trusted adult. They can help you figure out how to make sure it doesn't happen again.

INDEPENDENCE Day

I remember when I first got my learner's permit and was able to drive to see friends. I felt like I was finally living the main character life. Then, I was being careless one day and didn't put the parking brake on. I rolled down the driveway of my house and nearly broke the fence by the backyard (a seven-foot-ish drop down). Yikes. Independence can be fun, freeing—and sometimes frightening.

Maybe you can walk to a friend's house or to school, or bike to the pizza place on your own. Maybe you just got a phone, or you're starting to buy your own clothes. Soon enough, you'll be driving too.

THE OFF-LEASH LIFE

As my parents would constantly remind me, with independence comes responsibility—the responsibility to stay safe, and the responsibility to let your parents know that you are, in fact, safe.

If I walked to a friend's house and came home on time, the next outing might be farther away. Maybe I could go to the mall with my friends. The more I showed my parents that I could be trusted, the more independence they gave me.

Sometimes it feels safer to travel in groups. Getting lost when you're alone can be stressful. Getting lost with a group of friends is an adventure!

Your parents may seem really annoying when you're ready to spread your wings. They may call or text you all the time, or they may track your every move. Try to remember that, to them, you're like a little puppy running off-leash for the first time, and both of you need time to get used to your free-ranging.

STRANGER DANGER

A lot of girls look older than they are. One day, you might find yourself getting some unwanted attention from older people. Not knowing if a stranger is merely annoying or actually dangerous, the best way to handle that kind of attention is by not engaging the other person at all.

If you're out and someone makes you feel unsafe, find a trustworthy grown-up. A safe person can be someone you know, a security guard, or a parent or caregiver with other children. Stay with that person until you no longer feel threatened. Don't worry about the creepy stranger's feelings in these situations. Your safety comes first.

SOCIAL MEDIA: The Good, the Bad, the Pretty, the Ugly

Getting your first phone is a huge milestone. My parents gave me a phone when I started walking to school by myself. They wanted to be sure I landed safely. Of course, I quickly began to use my phone for way more than just texting my parents.

Social media can be great for things like connecting with friends on Instagram or finding TikTok communities of people who love bulldogs or baking or whatever your interests are. You can keep up with friends who don't live nearby. Social media can also provide a platform for your thoughts and opinions—it's easy to be yourself online.

However, social media also has a dark side. It can be hard to unplug. You can start to value yourself by the number of likes you get or followers you have. You might compare your likes and followers to your friends' numbers and feel insecure. You may lose hours of your life checking to see how many likes you're getting on a post! Seeing other people's cool photos of them looking great and having fun can make you feel mega FOMO.

PUBERTY GOGGLES

WHAT YOU SEE:

WHAT'S REALLY HAPPENING:

It's important to remind yourself that social media isn't real. Likes and followers on an app don't equal real-life friendships and relationships. Photos and videos can be staged, filtered, and edited. If you really pay attention, you might notice, like I have, that spending time on social media can make you feel bad. Many studies have linked high social media use with increased rates of depression and anxiety.

CYBERBULLYING

Online, bullies can't throw fruit at you in the cafeteria, pull your hair, or shove you to the ground. Cyberbullying can be much more painful, actually. When I was in middle school and high school, cyberbullies would leave mean comments under IG posts, spread rumors about people online on anonymous accounts, and make group chats just to gossip about other girls. I've seen some really nasty stuff on YouTube comments and in gaming communities.

Sometimes cyberbullying is more subtle. A group of friends can make a new chat and exclude just one person. Or someone posts a photo of a group of friends, but one of the friends is cropped out. These slights can be painful and hard to ignore. These are the best ways to keep cyberbullies out of your life:

- Keep your social media pages private.
- Use the block button for anyone who makes mean comments or posts.
- Involve a trusted adult if cyberbullying continues.

SEXTING LASTS FOREVER

You know how when you walk on the beach, your footprints are erased by the next wave? Your digital footprint is nothing like that. Every action you take—every photo you post, every comment you make, every story you like—can be traced back to you. There's no way to erase your activity on the internet. Know that any time you post something online, it could stay "out there" forever. Your future friends, dates, employers, and schools may check your digital footprint. A good rule is not to post anything you wouldn't want them (or your grandmother) to see.

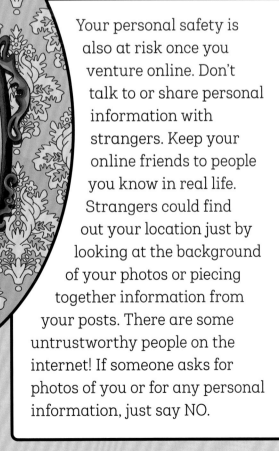

Your personal safety is also at risk once you venture online. Don't talk to or share personal information with strangers. Keep your online friends to people you know in real life. Strangers could find out your location just by looking at the background of your photos or piecing together information from your posts. There are some untrustworthy people on the internet! If someone asks for photos of you or for any personal information, just say NO.

GETTING AWAY FROM IT ALL

I try to take regular social media breaks. Sometimes I just have a lot of schoolwork, and it's embarrassing how much time can go by when I'm scrolling my Instagram feed. Sometimes I can actually feel my anxiety escalating, and I know it's time to unplug. If you are even a little bit curious, give it a try.

- **START WITH A GOAL.**
  Ask yourself: *Am I wasting time scrolling mindlessly? Am I feeling insecure because everyone else looks like they're having more fun?*

- **DECIDE HOW LONG YOU WANT YOUR BREAK TO BE:** a day, a week, forever?

- **LET YOUR FAMILY AND FRIENDS KNOW THAT YOU'RE TAKING A SOCIAL MEDIA DETOX.** Then delete your social media apps and/or temporarily disable your accounts.

- **TAKE ADVANTAGE OF ALL YOUR FREE TIME!** Paint, meditate, write in a journal. Hang out with friends *in person*! Read. Remember how to be alone.

Take note of how you feel when you're off social media. And if you like that feeling, maybe even keep it up.

SCHOOL—Not Just for Classes

For kids who excel, school can be a place where you learn interesting new things and build confidence. For other kids who struggle with learning or attentional issues, for people who have anxiety about taking tests or have a hard time keeping homework organized, school can feel like a special kind of hell. If you're a good student, good for you! If that's not you, then know that this is the only time of your life where you're expected to be good at everything. In college, in life, you can find the things you love and dive in.

WHAT DO YOU WANT TO DO?

Remember that your school experience doesn't take place only in the classroom. And you don't have to do just the things your friends like to do. This is the time to find your own path! Join a club, play a sport, audition for a play or choir. Take an after-school pottery class or learn how to play guitar.

So many things about growing and changing are challenging. *This*–figuring out who you are and what you enjoy–is the fun part!

Becoming a CITIZEN of the WORLD

What matters to you? What moves you to take action? What changes do you want to make to your world? As you become aware of the people and the world around you beyond your home and school, you will start asking yourself some big questions.

There are a lot of things to stand up for, whether it's nature conservation or racial equality. I found my political voice in middle school—I cared about the fight against climate change, and I cared about making women feel safe and heard in America. I started by reposting useful information on Twitter and Instagram. (Very important to check sources before you re-post stuff, by the way.) I joined my school's Asian culture club, where we talked about current issues and organized school events. My hometown friends and I founded a nonprofit student volunteer group with the help of our parents, where we organized a Stop Asian Hate march and town-wide events about climate change. I learned that there were a lot of things I could do to make my community a better place, even as a teen. In fact, people listened more because I was a teen. Nothing has ever made me feel more powerful than using my voice!

Am I WEIRD???

I DON'T HAVE A FRIEND GROUP.

It's normal to have times and be in places when you feel like you can't connect with anybody. There will be moments where you feel alone and friendless throughout your life. Those moments won't last forever, though—you will meet new people who will make you laugh and feel loved.

I DON'T LIKE MY FRIENDS.

Nobody likes their friends all the time. And a lot of people wind up in a friend group where they don't like a lot of things about a lot of the people in that group, but they get a bit lazy about changing it up. Friendship can be complicated, and it's not weird if you feel that way. Still, it's nice to have a friend or two who you do connect with in some way. Broaden your circle. Maybe that girl who has really smart things to say in English class, or the one who has awesome doodles in her notebook, or the one who wears great thrift store clothes—the one you never considered as a friend before—might be someone you do like.

I *LIKE* TO BE ALONE!

You are *awesome* if you like to be alone. A lot of teenagers don't know how to just be, or to be with themselves. You are way ahead of the game.

I DON'T KNOW WHAT I WANT TO DO WITH MY LIFE.
You have plenty of time to figure that out! Some people decide when they are five years old that they want to be an artist or a scientist. Some people try a lot of different things into their 20s or 30s even before they figure it out. Keep an open mind and you will find your bliss.

I'M NOT ON SOCIAL MEDIA.
You are less likely to feel depressed or anxious than your peers who are on social media. And you are absolutely not missing anything.

Things I Wished I'd Known When I Was Going Through PUBERTY...

Having made it through the minefield of puberty unscathed, here's just a little bit of "wrapping it all up" advice that may make your road less bumpy and more enjoyable.

SLOW DOWN

I rushed through middle school and a lot of high school because I wanted to become a grown-up as fast as I could. I felt like being a kid was lame. I tried acting cool by avoiding "childish" or "cringey" stuff, and thought I could be totally independent before I was fully ready to be on my own. I wish I'd known a lot of things when I was 12. I wish I'd known to spend more time with my grandparents, and I wish I'd learned a Korean recipe or two from them. And, perhaps most importantly, I wish I'd known to enjoy being a kid and the growing pains that come with it.

WHAT SEEMS LIKE A BIG DEAL . . . IS NOT

When I was in middle school, there was nonstop drama with my friends. Every slight and fight felt like the end of the world. But with even just a little bit of perspective, those problems that seemed overwhelming, the ones that gave me stomachaches and kept me up at night, seem so petty and meaningless now. I wish I had understood, back then, how easy it was to just walk away from the people who make you crazy.

BE HERE NOW

I spent much of puberty waiting for it to be over. I was tired of the in-between stage of being too old to act like a child and too much of a child to be thought of as a mature adult. It wasn't until the end of high school that I realized how valuable my experiences and relationships were in my teen years, because they helped to form my perspective of the world. I wish that I would have taken more time to appreciate all I had, and all I already was, instead of constantly wondering, "what if . . . ?" You'll never be the age you are now again, so try to embrace it.

RESOURCES

WEBSITES

girlshealth.gov for tools and tips

mindfulnessforteens.com for guided meditations

teenshealth.org for health information

teenhelp.com for general information

teenlineonline.org for mental health support

BOOKS

My Anxious Mind: A Teen's Guide to Managing Anxiety and Panic by Michael A. Tompkins and Katherine Martinez

Girl Activist by Louisa Kamps, Susanna Daniel and Michelle Wildgen

TED TALKS

Insight Into the Teenage Brain, TEDx Talk by Adriana Galván

Questions Every Teenager Needs to be Asked, TEDx Talk by Laurence Lewars

CRISIS LINES

The Trevor Lifeline:
Call 1-866-488-7386
and thetrevorproject.org
provide 24/7 counseling for LGBTQ youth

Suicide and Crisis Lifeline: Call 988

Crisis Textline: Text CONNECT to 741741 for immediate, free, 24/7 help with anxiety